Lacy Sunshine's
Flower Pot Pretties Coloring Book Volume 6

Magical and Adorable Bloomin' Fairy Beauties

**Illustrated by Artist
Heather Valentin**

©Heather Valentin. www.lacysunshine.weebly.com 2015
All Rights Reserved. Personal Use Only. No Redistribution.

This Flower Pot Pretties Coloring Book Belongs To

_____

Made in the USA
Lexington, KY
20 March 2017